Originally published as
La Via della Croce verso la Pasqua, copyright © 1997
Editoriale Jaca Book spa, Milan.

English translation copyright © 1997
by Wm. B. Eerdmans Publishing Co.
255 Jefferson Ave. S.E., Grand Rapids, Mich. 49503/
P.O. Box 163, Cambridge CB3 9PU U.K.

Printed in Italy

Library of Congress Cataloging-in-Publication Data

Biffi, Inos.
[The way of the cross.   English]
The Way of the Cross
text by Inos Biffi; illustrations by Franco Vignazia.
p.   cm.
ISBN 0-8028-5135-5

Imprimatur
in Curia Arch. Mediolani die 17 Julii 1996
Angelus Mascheroni
provicarius generalis

INOS BIFFI is Professor of Medieval
and Systematic Theology at the
Theological University of Northern Italy, Milan.

FRANCO VIGNAZIA lives in Italy
and is an illustrator, painter,
and sculptor. He also teaches
art in the secondary schools.

Unless otherwise indicated, all
Scripture quotations
are from the New American Bible,
© 1986 Confraternity of Christian
Doctrine, Washington, D.C.

The Way of the Cross

Holy Week, the Stations of the Cross, and the Resurrection

Text by Inos Biffi

Illustrations by Franco Vignazia

WILLIAM B. EERDMANS PUBLISHING COMPANY
GRAND RAPIDS, MICHIGAN

Contents

Introduction

This book has been written and illustrated as a children's guide to the celebration of Holy Week, which begins with Palm Sunday and concludes with Easter Sunday. During these days of the liturgical year, the Church recalls with special fervor the events of the Lord's life — in particular, his suffering, his death, his burial, and his resurrection. This commemoration enkindles a more intense, ardent prayer, and the rites of the liturgy become more solemn and striking.

Children should be taught to participate in at least some of these rites. (It would be too difficult for them to attend all of them.) This participation will help them to understand the liturgical rites and experience their powerful impact, and so begin to appreciate them.

This book will help them, first through its illustrations, which portray with strong and lively clarity the scriptural accounts that the Church reads during Holy Week. The pictures will offer an attractive introduction to the events that are recalled and represented during Holy Week. But the pictures could be confusing if there were no words. Hence the text, which explains what the Scripture recounts and what the Church's celebration commemorates and relives.

You will also find in these pages the stations of the Cross, or *Via crucis* (the Way of the Cross), the sorrowful path toward the resurrection. The stations are also illustrated, and can be done by the children before Easter. But they will be accompanied by their parents, their catechists, and, in general, those adults who by instruction and witness act as attentive and persuasive teachers of the faith. This form of instruction for children will have an advantage for adults, too: they will find their own faith growing and becoming more mature.

Holy Week
The Entrance into Jerusalem

Among all the weeks of the year, one in particular is called "holy." This is the week that commemorates the Passover of Christ: his passion, death, and resurrection.

Holy Week opens on a joyful note with Palm Sunday, which commemorates Jesus' entrance into Jerusalem. A huge crowd of rejoicing people accompanies Jesus, who is seated on a colt. They spread out cloaks and leafy branches along the way, and they greet Jesus as the meek and blessed king "who comes in the name of the Lord."

But the gladness of that day is mixed with sorrow, with weeping. It is Jesus who weeps. Looking out on the city, Jesus cannot hold back his tears at the thought that one day soon, because of its unbelief, the city will be besieged and destroyed, along with its inhabitants. Even the applause he is now hearing will change in a few days' time into a noisy and senseless demand for his condemnation. After the way of triumph comes the Way of the Cross.

The Preparation of the Upper Room

For the Jews, the most solemn of Holy Days is Passover. During the Passover they relive their liberation from slavery under Pharaoh, their miraculous exodus from Egypt, and their journey to the Promised Land, a journey on which God lovingly accompanied them and showed them every kindness.

Every year Jesus also takes part in the Passover supper. The one he is about to celebrate will be his last. It is also the one he has longed for most of all, because now his Body will take the place of the unleavened bread, the cup of his Blood will replace the cup of wine, and he himself, in the place of the Passover lamb, will become "the Lamb of God, who takes away the sin of the world" (John 1:29).

Everything has to be ready for the ceremony. Two of the disciples take care of this part. At Jesus' command they prepare a big room furnished with couches for the banquet. The room is in the upper story of a house lent by an acquaintance of the Master. But as we shall see, another one of the disciples, Judas, has also been busy — plotting Jesus' betrayal.

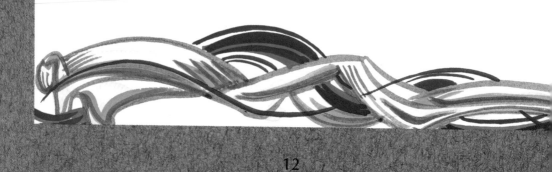

The Washing of the Feet

Before the meal, after Jesus has wrapped a towel around his waist, he performs the humble service of washing his disciples' feet, just as if he were a slave. This act upsets the disciples and arouses their opposition. Peter speaks for them when he at first protests Jesus' gesture, but Jesus warns him: to refuse to have his feet washed is to refuse the humiliation of the Cross, from which alone salvation comes. And what is more, the disciples themselves will have to imitate Jesus' behavior. They will have to put themselves at one another's service, choosing, as Jesus did, the last place.

The Last Supper

For the last time, Jesus gathers with his disciples to commemorate how God liberated the people through the Passover. For the last time, he will break the unleavened bread, drink the wine from the cup, and eat the lamb seasoned with bitter herbs.

But the old Passover has come to an end for the disciples, too. When Jesus says, "Take and eat; this is my

body," and "Drink from it, all of you, for this is my blood of the covenant, which will be shed . . . for the forgiveness of sins" (Matt. 26:26-27), he establishes the Eucharist as a new Passover. And when we celebrate the Eucharist in obedience to his command — "Do this in memory of me" (Luke 22:19) — we find there the sacrifice that Jesus accomplished on the Cross. We receive Jesus' boundless love for all humankind, and we renew our hope for his coming.

The Eucharist is the Church's Passover. Every year, on Holy Thursday — the Thursday of Holy Week — we commemorate how Jesus gave the Church the Eucharist at the Last Supper.

The Mount of Olives

After the Passover meal and the institution of the
Eucharist, Jesus, accompanied by his disciples, leaves the
Upper Room to spend the night in prayer on the Mount
of Olives. Jesus knows that his death is immediately at
hand; racked with anguish, he cries out, "My soul is
sorrowful even to death" (Matt. 26:38). Jesus' sorrow is so
great that his sweat becomes like drops of blood, but he
prays more and more intensely. He calls on the Father to
set him free from death, all the while entrusting himself
completely to the Father: "My Father, if it is possible, let
this cup" — this death — "pass from me; yet, not as I will,

but as you will" (Matt. 26:39). Nearby are Peter, James, and John, who have fallen asleep. Meanwhile, an angel comes down from heaven to comfort Jesus. Everyone terrified by death discovers they are close to Jesus.

We commemorate Jesus' agony on the night between Holy Thursday and Good Friday.

The Betrayal

Judas had already been planning to betray Jesus for a while now. From the time Judas realized that Jesus would not experience a glorious end and that *this* Messiah wouldn't bring him power and money, he began to lose faith in Jesus. Jesus had been aware of this ever since Judas had refused to accept him as the Bread come down from heaven.

Then, as the Last Supper approached, "Satan entered into Judas" (Luke 22:3), and for thirty pieces of silver he promised to hand Jesus over to the leaders of the people.

After that, he remained a part of the group of the twelve disciples, but "he was a thief and held the money bag and used to steal the contributions" (John 12:6). Judas also took part in the Last Supper and perhaps received the Eucharist. But then, driven by the devil that dwelt in his heart, Judas went out into the night and with a kiss — the sign of friendship — betrayed Jesus to the crowd that had come armed with clubs to arrest him on the Mount of Olives. Afterwards, Judas was filled with remorse: he gave back the money and went off to hang himself. But we can be sure that Jesus never stopped loving him and offering him forgiveness.

Annas   Caiaphas

Jesus' Trial

After his arrest, Jesus has to
undergo a very painful trial, based
entirely on lies. First he is led
before the high priests Annas and
Caiaphas and accused by false
witnesses. Jesus declares that he is
the Son of God; his judges find
him guilty, deserving of death, and
he is spat upon and slapped.

That night, Peter denies Jesus

Herod

Pilate

out of fear, swearing that he doesn't even know Jesus —
who had foretold it all: "Before the cock crows, you will
deny me three times" (Matt. 26:34). As soon as Peter
remembers Jesus' words, he goes out and weeps bitterly.

The next morning, the judges take Jesus to Pilate, the
Roman governor, whom they want to pronounce the death
sentence. Pilate, in turn, sends Jesus to Herod, the king
of Galilee, but Jesus does not answer him a single word.
When Jesus is led back to Pilate, the Jews want Barabbas,
a notorious prisoner, to be released instead of the Lord.

"Behold, the Man!"

"I am a king," Jesus says, answering a question from Pilate, but adds, "My kingdom does not belong to this world" (John 18:36-37). Jesus' words are met with mockery. In order to make fun of him, the soldiers weave a crown of thorns and put it on his head; they dress him up in a fancy cloak — to mimic the cloaks that kings wear — and put a reed in his right hand as a scepter. Then they come before him saying, "Hail, King of the Jews!" (John 19:3).

Next, Pilate presents Jesus to the crowd: "Behold, the man!" (John 19:5), "Behold, your king!" The inscription that Pilate himself later orders to be posted on the Cross will read: "Jesus the Nazorean,

the King of the Jews"
(John 19:19). No one, of
course, would be able to
recognize that this man,
with his ridiculous and
humiliating costume, was
a true king. He could
only be a crazy fool. Yet
he really was a King, the
only King, and his
resurrection from death
would reveal his kingship.
Until then, only faith
could recognize him as
a King. Or, as Jesus tells
Pilate, "Everyone who
belongs to the truth
listens to my voice"
(John 18:37).

The First Station

Jesus Is Condemned

Pilate has mockingly called Jesus a king, but he does not seriously acknowledge Jesus' kingship. Though he finds no guilt in Jesus, Pilate is afraid that he will lose his position if he does not condemn Jesus. So Pilate has him flogged and then, when he has washed his hands of the matter like a coward, orders Jesus' death.

For Jesus, this is the beginning of what in Latin we call the *Via crucis:* the Way of the Cross. The death sentence is the first "station," a word which means "a stopping-place on the journey to the Cross." Now we are going to accompany Jesus on this sorrowful journey and relive his sorrow in our hearts.

The Second Station

Jesus Is Made to Carry the Cross

"Away with him, away with him! Crucify him!" When the people shout these words, Pilate hands Jesus over to be crucified. The soldiers strip him of his fancy cloak, put his clothes back on him, and lift the Cross onto his shoulders. Then they lead him toward "the Place of the Skull" — Calvary. Now we are at the second station of the Way of the Cross. Here we behold the Son of God in the form of a poor condemned man: Crushed by a burden too heavy to carry, he sets us free from the heavy burden of our sins.

The Third Station
Jesus Falls for the First Time

At the third station, we look upon Jesus, unable to bear the weight of the Cross, as he falls for the first time along the way. The Gospel does not mention that Jesus fell down, but we have good reason to believe that he did. After all, the wood of the Cross was crushingly heavy, and Jesus had been greatly weakened by his agony and by the blows he had received. This fall represents and comforts all those broken by suffering.

The Fourth Station
Jesus Meets His Mother

At the foot of the Cross, on Calvary, we will find Mary. But we can be sure that she has not left Jesus alone even during this painful journey. Even if the disciples have abandoned him out of fear, his mother is still close to him with her tender love. As far back as Jesus' presentation in the temple, Simeon had foretold that a sword would pierce Mary's heart — and her son's death is that sword.

Mary's consoling presence is always there to comfort all who suffer. This fourth station assures us of that.

The Fifth Station
Simon of Cyrene

Jesus cannot continue carrying the Cross alone, so a passerby is forced to help him. This is how the Gospel tells the story: "As they led him away they took hold of a certain Simon, a Cyrenian, who was coming in from the country; and after laying the cross on him, they

made him carry it behind Jesus" (Luke 23:26).

The fifth station shows us that we are called to become — not by constraint, but out of love — helpful companions and sincere friends of our brothers and sisters, bringing them relief in body and in spirit.

The Sixth Station
Veronica and the Face of Jesus

A huge crowd of people and of women follow Jesus as he carries the Cross. It is believed that one of these women, by the name of Veronica, approached Jesus and, in an act of loving devotion, wiped his holy face, which was dripping with blood. The story goes that the image of Jesus' face was miraculously imprinted on the linen cloth.

At the sixth station, we reflect on this woman's thoughtfulness and compassion, in order that we too may learn to wipe the faces of our brothers and sisters who are sick and afflicted.

The Seventh Station
Jesus Falls for the Second Time

Jesus falls again. He is worn out. He is not only exhausted in his body and no longer able to stand up straight. Above all, he is humiliated and cast down by our sins, which weigh heavily on his soul. At the seventh station, we think about Jesus, the Lamb of God who carries the world's sin on his shoulders. And we ask to be forgiven for contributing, with our sins, to making Jesus fall on the way to Calvary.

The Eighth Station
The Devout Women

A large number of women follow Jesus along the Way of the Cross, beating their breasts and lamenting over him. But Jesus tells them to shed tears not for him but for themselves and for their children because of the great misfortunes that one day soon will rain down upon his people. Jerusalem will be destroyed, and many, many Jews will perish. At the eighth station, these words are a burning summons to us to weep for our sins and to be ready to welcome the gift of salvation.

The Ninth Station
Jesus Falls for the Third Time

Before reaching Calvary, Jesus falls a third time. At the ninth station of the *Via crucis,* we contemplate this third fall. The Son of God is reduced to the lowest point of humiliation. Now our thoughts go back to something that he said on the eve of his passion: "Amen, amen, I say to you, unless a grain of wheat falls to the ground and dies, it remains just a grain of wheat; but if it dies, it produces much fruit" (John 12:24). Indeed, after being buried, Jesus will rise again as Lord, and his death will bear fruit — the salvation of the world.

The Tenth Station
Jesus Is Stripped of His Garments

Jesus has reached Calvary, a small, skull-shaped outcropping of rock. There the soldiers strip him of his clothes, which they divide into four shares, one for each soldier. Jesus also has a seamless tunic, woven from top to bottom in a single piece. Rather than tear it apart, the soldiers cast lots for it. Jesus appears on the Cross absolutely poor, but through his poverty we receive true riches — his love. He once proclaimed that the poor are blessed; Jesus crucified is first among the poor.

The Eleventh Station
Jesus Is Nailed to the Cross

Once at Calvary, the soldiers nail Jesus to the Cross that Simon
has carried. Also being crucified are two criminals, one at Jesus'
right and one at his left. As we already know, the soldiers place
over Jesus' head the written charges against him: "Jesus the
Nazorean, King of the Jews." Jesus will remain on the Cross from
noon until three in the afternoon, being mocked and cursed. Yet
Jesus answers not with vengeful words but with words of
forgiveness for everyone — even for
the good thief, to whom
he promises paradise.

The Twelfth Station
Jesus Dies

During Jesus' three hours of agony, a great darkness descends over the earth. Meanwhile, Jesus prays intensely. He recites the Psalm that begins with the words "My God, my God, why have you forsaken me?" (Matt. 27:46), entrusting himself completely to the Father: "Father, into your hands I commend my spirit" (Luke 23:46). At the end, when God's work has been accomplished, Jesus cries out in a loud voice and surrenders his spirit. As he dies, the earth quakes and the rocks split apart. At this very hour, the Passover lambs are being sacrificed in the temple. But the true lamb is Jesus, who also meets his death with bones unbroken. On Good Friday, our loving, grateful gaze is completely focused on the Crucified One.

Mary, Our Mother

The person who gazed most attentively at Jesus on the Cross during those hours of horrible agony was the Virgin Mary. On Calvary, Simeon's prophecy that a sword would pierce her heart comes true. The Evangelist John writes that "when Jesus saw his mother and the disciple there whom he loved, he said to his mother, 'Woman, behold, your son.' Then he said to the disciple, 'Behold, your mother.' And from that hour the disciple took her into his home" (John 19:26-27).

In welcoming Jesus' favorite disciple, Mary

welcomes all the Lord's disciples as her own children. In the same way, that disciple stands for all his fellow disciples when he takes Mary into his own home.

On the evening of the Last Supper, Jesus left us his Body and his Blood. From the Cross, before he dies, he entrusts us to the person whom he has loved and still loves more than anyone else on earth: his mother. He does this so that we also may receive from her the same maternal tenderness and protection.

The Thirteenth Station
Jesus Is Taken Down from the Cross

"When it was evening," Matthew writes, "there came a rich man from Arimathea, named Joseph, who was himself a disciple of Jesus. He went to Pilate and asked for the body of Jesus; then Pilate ordered it to be handed over" (Matt. 27:57-58). At the thirteenth station, we imagine Jesus' lifeless body laid on Mary's lap. A very old prayer arises from our hearts: "Holy Virgin, you counted all the blows of sin in the wounds of Jesus. With filial love I want to stay at your side and share your grief."

The Fourteenth Station
Jesus Is Placed in the Tomb

Joseph of Arimathea takes Jesus' body and, with the help of Nicodemus, the man who had gone to visit the Master secretly one night, binds it with linen cloths along with spices. John describes the burial of Jesus: "Now in the place where he had been crucified there was a garden, and in the garden a new tomb, in which no one had yet been buried. . . . So they laid Jesus there" (John 19:41-42). Fearing that the disciples might steal the Lord's body, the Jews convince Pilate to secure the tomb. Pilate has the stone that covers the entrance sealed and then stations guards to watch over it. It seems that everything is over, the way it seems when any person is buried.

We spend Holy Saturday at the tomb. But we are waiting. On the third day, it will open again to give us Christ, now risen and glorious.

The *Via crucis* is over. But the fourteenth station is followed by another: the Sunday of the Resurrection.

The Resurrection
Jesus Rises from the Dead

The tomb doesn't keep Jesus' body long enough for it to decay. As Jesus himself had foretold, on the third day he rises again from death. The tomb is left empty, with an angel keeping watch. Here is how the Gospel tells it: "After the sabbath, as the first day of the week was dawning . . . there was a great earthquake; for an angel of the Lord descended from heaven, approached, rolled back the stone, and sat upon it. His appearance was like lightning and his clothing was white as snow. The guards were shaken with fear of him and became like dead men" (Matt. 28:1-4).

Now Jesus is risen and alive. The Church proclaims this to us at the Easter Vigil. Through the merits of Jesus, death, which is the fruit of sin, has been conquered forever. The Father has heard the prayer of his obedient Son. The

Cross, once a
shameful gallows,
has become the
triumphant Lord's
trophy of a glorious
victory. The Crucified
One reigns in glory.

Innocence has
sprung forth in the
world, joy has blos-
somed again, hope
has been reborn, and
sinful people have
become beloved
children of God.

We now wait for
the Lord to "come
to judge the living
and the dead."

Easter Morning

The sabbath is over. The women come to the tomb early in the morning, bringing fragrant spices to carefully complete the anointing of Jesus' body, performed in haste the night of the burial. But they find the tomb empty. It is watched over by an angel, who says to them, "Do not be afraid! I know that you are seeking Jesus the crucified. He is not here, for he has been raised just as he said. Come and see the place where he lay" (Matt. 28:5-6). Caught up in fear and wonder, but also overflowing with joy, the women hurry to bring the disciples the news of this happy event. Along the way, however, Jesus comes to meet them in person. They bow down to the ground before him and cling to his feet. He tells them to be glad: "Rejoice — do not be afraid."

When Mary Magdalene comes to the tomb, she is even more distressed to find it empty. Convinced that Jesus' body has been stolen, she searches for it anxiously, in tears. She does not realize that Jesus himself is near her — she thinks he is the gardener. But as soon as he calls her by name, she recognizes him and embraces him. Then she runs to the disciples and announces, "I have seen the Lord" (John 20:18).

Emmaus

After Jesus' crucifixion, it had seemed that everything had come to a wretched end. There was nothing left for the two disciples from Emmaus to do but to go back home, taking their bitterness and disappointment with them.

But then, along the way, the risen Jesus comes up to them and walks with them — except they don't recognize him. They mistake him for a common wayfarer, and they tell him all about their bitterness and discouragement over the pitiful end of Jesus the Nazorean, "a prophet mighty in deed and word" who was sentenced to death and hung on a cross. "But we were hoping that he would be the one to redeem Israel," they lament (Luke 24:21), as if to say that hope has been extinguished in their hearts, and that the rumors about Jesus' resurrection haven't been enough to rekindle it. Surprisingly, this chance companion now begins to scold them, calling them "foolish" and "slow of heart" (Luke 24:25) for not grasping that, according to Moses and the Prophets, Christ *had* to suffer and so enter into his glory. Since it is nearly evening, the two disciples invite this mysterious traveler to stay with them. At supper, when he breaks bread, they recognize him as the risen Lord, but he immediately vanishes from their sight. The two promptly set out for Jerusalem, where they find that by now all the Apostles and disciples are convinced that Jesus is truly risen. This is our conviction, too: Through his presence in the Word and in the Eucharist, the Lord continues to accompany the Church on her journey until the end of time.

Words of the Risen Lord

"Do not be afraid."
(Matt. 28:9)

"Woman, why are you weeping? Whom are
you looking for?"
(John 20:15)

"Peace be with you. As the Father has sent me,
so I send you."
(John 20:21)

"Receive the Holy Spirit. Whose sins you forgive
are forgiven them."
(John 20:22-23)

"Do not be unbelieving, but believe."
(John 20:27)

"Blessed are those who have not seen and
have believed."
(John 20:29)

"Proclaim the Gospel to every creature."
(Mark 16:15)

"Whoever believes and is baptized
will be saved."
(Mark 16:16)

"And behold, I am with you always, until the
end of the age."
(Matt. 28:20)